How to Handle Sexual Harassment in the Workplace During the #MeToo Era

A Guide for Employees and Managers

Beth K. Whittenbury, J.D.

Kolbury Press

Published by Kolbury Press

This work provides a guide to understanding some legal concepts. However, nothing in this book may be relied upon as legal advice. For specific advice, please contact a licensed attorney in your state.

Library of Congress Control Number: 2020909474

ISBN-13: 978-0-9979019-3-1

Other books by Beth K. Whittenbury include: Investigating the Workplace Harassment Complaint, American Bar Association Publishing, © 2012, available at: www.ShopABA.org. and A Manager's Guide to Preventing Liability for Sexual Harassment in the Workplace, © 2013, available through online booksellers.

DEDICATION

This book is dedicated to all those who have dealt with sexual harassment in the workplace. May it play, at least, a small role in helping to end unfairness in the workplace.

Beth K. Whittenbury

CONTENTS

PREFACE

This book is designed as a quick read for managers, supervisors, and aspiring business students who need to understand their liability and responsibilities with respect to issues of sexual harassment in the workplace. It is also designed to explain the rights of workers to remain free from illegal harassment. Although a previous version of this book was published in 2013, *A Manager's Guide to Preventing Liability for Sexual Harassment in the Workplace,* the dawn and effulgence of the #MeToo Era has necessitated a new version, one which traces the history of sexual harassment and allows workers to understand how current law affects and protects them. Many of the passages in this book can also be found in the previous book, but here you find an expanded edition with a broader focus.

Where California law differs from federal law, the author notes the differences. If you work outside of California, the laws of your state may differ somewhat from those set forth below. However, most states follow federal law fairly closely. California, in general, has stricter guidelines than federal law. Managers should always work to the highest standard and not try to do the minimum required. Therefore, all supervisors and managers will benefit from a discussion of the higher standards applied in California. Workers in other states should check their state's laws to see whether their state standards differ from what is explained in this book.

All law is ever-changing and developing. Also, the commentary in this book is not case-specific. Therefore, nothing in this book can be relied upon as legal advice. For case-specific responses or for legal advice you should contact your own attorney or your company's legal department.

So without further ado, let's jump in!

CHAPTER 1

THE HISTORY OF SEXUAL HARASSMENT IN THE WORKPLACE

Prior to 1964, sexual harassment was legal in the workplace. In fact, think about the old movies you sometimes watch on late night television. Those movies frequently depict male bosses calling their female secretaries "Honey," "Sweetheart," "Precious," or "Angel" and resting their hands on the knees of their secretaries or worse. Review *The Maltese Falcon*, if you don't believe me. What's even more startling now is that the secretary in that movie appeared to like it! My own grandmother was literally chased around the desk by her boss. I can tell you that she didn't like it! These situations were real and prevalent. There was no law to prevent it or to stop it.

Sexual harassment as a form of sex discrimination was first prohibited in employment situations by Title VII of the Civil Rights Act of 1964. The drafters of the bill that eventually became the Civil Rights Act of 1964 did not originally intend to include sex as a category protected from discrimination in employment, since they primarily focused on addressing racial injustice. As originally drafted, it forbid discrimination based on race, religion, color, creed, and national origin. Apparently no one felt it necessary to protect women from discrimination in the workplace. In fact, sex was added to the bill as a protected category in an effort to block passage of the bill. A southern senator who was against prohibiting racial discrimination added sex as a protected category figuring that an all-male congress, which Congress was at that time, would never vote to outlaw discrimination in the workplace based on sex.

Apparently, the joke was on him, because the law passed in spite of his amendment added to defeat it, and sex became a category protected from discrimination in the workplace. In fact, the bill passed without much discussion of the amendment adding sex as a protected category. So, it's not too surprising then that this part of the law was largely ignored for decades.

It wasn't until 1986 that the US Supreme Court, in a case called *Meritor v. Vinson*[1], finally ruled that sexual harassment is a cause of action under the Civil Rights Act of 1964, specifically Title VII of that Act. Until then, lower court opinions had been split with some finding that these "problems" were just of an interpersonal nature between two people not getting along and other courts holding that these "problems" were prohibited discrimination as a matter of law. In *Meritor v. Vinson*, the US Supreme Court reasoned that the female secretaries in the case would not have received propositions from their male bosses if those secretaries had been male. Therefore, the female secretaries were being treated differently because of their sex, and that behavior constituted illegal discrimination under Title VII of the Civil Rights Act of 1964. It was a landmark case and one still oft-quoted today.

Of interesting note, Anita Hill claimed, in 1991, that Clarence Thomas had sexually harassed her ten years before when he had been the head of the Equal Employment Opportunity Commission ("EEOC"), the federal agency responsible for enforcing Title VII of the Civil Rights Act of 1964. Ten years before 1991 is 1981, five years prior to the US Supreme Court Decision in *Meritor v. Vinson*. The timing could account for the fact that Ms. Hill did not file a formal complaint at the time of the incidents.

[1] Meritor Savings Bank v. Vinson, 477 U.S. 57 (1986).

After the passage of the federal Civil Rights Act, states began to pass their own versions of anti-discrimination laws. Most of these largely mirror Title VII of the federal Civil Rights Act of 1964. Some states have chosen to protect more categories from discrimination than find protection at the federal level. California has one of the more exhaustive lists of categories shielded from discrimination in employment. California's anti-workplace discrimination law is mostly found in its Fair Employment and Housing Act codified within its Government Code.

Anita Hill's testimony shined a light on the problem of sexual harassment in the workplace and spawned an uptick in claims under both federal and state laws. Although many people thought these claims would dissipate over time, they did not. In an attempt to stem the tide, legislatures began passing more laws aimed at preventing sexual harassment from occurring, and courts rendered more opinions clarifying what was and wasn't appropriate behavior within workplaces. Studies promulgated to try and understand why these problems persisted, producing some notable findings.

Older studies showed that, in general, women have the opposite reactions to certain types of sexually-based behavior than men. For example, more women found propositions offensive than didn't, while more men than not found propositions flattering.[2] Some courts, looking at that data, began to formulate standards, for determining whether sexual harassment had occurred, that allowed for those different perspectives among the sexes.[3] In 1994, the Merit Systems Protection Board reported that forty-four percent of women and nineteen percent of men had experienced sexual harassment in employment.[4] A perusal of EEOC reports during the relevant years

---

[2] Konrad, A. M., & Gutek, B. A. (1986). Impact of work experiences on attitudes toward sexual harassment. Administrative Science Quarterly, 31, 422-438.

[3] See *Ellison v. Brady*, 924. F.2d 872 (9th Cir. 1991).

[4] U.S. Merit Systems Protection Board, Sexual Harassment in the Federal Workplace: Trends, Progress, Continuing Challenges (1994) available at

shows the percentage of sexual harassment claims by men to have doubled between 1990 and 2009.[5] Since sexual harassment claims continued to rise, some states began implementing training requirements for supervisors. For example, in 2004, California passed a law, modeled on a Connecticut statute, requiring that employers with fifty or more employees provide all supervisors two hours of sexual harassment training every two years.

Still, sexual harassment persisted even in the most progressive states. More troubling was the documented trend that employees experiencing sexual harassment failed to report or address it for fear of shame or outright retaliation. A 2003 survey found that 75% of those who reported sexual harassment in the workplace were subjected to some form of retaliation.[6] According to the 2016 EEOC Select Task Force on the Study of Harassment in the Workplace, "The least common response to harassment is to take some formal action – either to report the harassment internally or file a formal legal complaint."[7]

http://www.mspb.gov/netsearch/viewdocs.aspx?docnumber=253661&version=2 53948 (last visited 4/21/20).
[5] See https://www.vox.com/identities/2017/10/15/16438750/weinstein-sexual-harassment-facts stating: "According to the EEOC, reports of men experiencing workplace sexual assault have nearly doubled between 1990 and 2009, from 8 percent to 16 percent of all claims."
[6] Lilia M. Cortina & Vicki J. Magley, Raising Voice, Risking Retaliation: Events Following Interpersonal Mistreatment in the Workplace, 8:4 J. OCCUPATIONAL HEALTH PSYCHOL. 247, 255 (2003).
[7] Report of the Co-Chairs of The EEOC Select Task Force on the Study of Harassment in the Workplace 2016 at 6; https://www.eeoc.gov/eeoc/task_force/harassment/upload/report.pdf.

The number of claims each year did not appreciably decline, and surveys continued to show that more men and women experienced sexual harassment at work than complained or filed law suits to address it.[8]

---

[8] See Lilia M. Cortina and Jennifer L. Berdahl, Sexual Harassment in Organizations: A Decade of Research in Review, 1 THE SAGE HANDBOOK OF ORGANIZATIONAL BEHAVIOR 469, 469-96 (J. Barling & C. L. Cooper eds., 2008); https://www.umass.edu/employmentequity/employers-responses-sexual-harassment (Last visited 4/18/2020) (stating that "The overwhelming majority (99.8%) of people who experience sexual harassment at work never file formal charges.") University of Massachusetts Amherst, Center for Employment Equity 2018 Report.

Beth K. Whittenbury

CHAPTER 2

THE RISE OF THE #METOO ERA

In February of 2017, something amazing happened. A woman in Silicon Valley posted a blog entry that somehow cut open the cone of silence which had keep stories of sexual harassment private and started women saying, publicly, "That happened to me too!" Her name is Susan Fowler, a former employee of Uber. With the innocuous title "Reflecting On One Very, Very Strange Year At Uber," the blog post chronicled the sexual harassment Ms. Fowler experienced at Uber while an employee there and Uber's failure to adequately respond or protect her despite its knowledge and her repeated complaints.[9]

Ms. Fowler received public comments on her blog, essentially saying that those commenting had experienced similar sexual harassment. Some had experienced it at Uber, some even with the same supervisor at Uber, while others had experienced analogous behavior at other Silicon Valley employers. Venture Capitalists seemed among the largest offenders, but many Silicon Valley employers suddenly found their employees publicly outing behavior that had gone

---

[9] https://www.susanjfowler.com/blog/2017/2/19/reflecting-on-one-very-strange-year-at-uber (Last visited 4/18/20)

on unchecked for years.[10]

The public outrage unleashed in Silicon Valley eventually wended its way to Hollywood and in October of 2017, Alyssa Milano posted her now famous tweet, "If you've been sexually harassed or assaulted write 'me too' as a reply to this tweet." Overnight, her tweet went viral and the #MeToo Movement was born.

It turns out that Alyssa Milano was not the first to use the term "Me Too." The term or "movement" originated in 2006 by a woman named Tarana Burke, who founded a non-profit to help victims of sexual assault and harassment find pathways to healing. Apparently, Alyssa Milano's celebrity status catapulted the already existing MeToo Movement to national attention. The overwhelming response to Ms. Milano's tweet showed the depth and pervasiveness of the problem. By the following Academy Awards season, so many Hollywood celebrities had joined the cause that they banded together to form the #TimesUp legal defense fund.

The efforts of Tarana Burke, Susan Fowler, and Alyssa Milano miraculously emboldened many people to publicly speak out on an issue which they had previously mostly kept to themselves. It appears that an unemotional, factual blog post, by someone not seeking any personal gain, may have been the catalyst people were waiting for to make their experiences with sexual harassment known. Suddenly, the issue came into broad daylight, and new surveys showing the appalling prevalence of sexual harassment and sexual assault were published. For example, a 2018 survey from Stop Street Harassment showed eighty-one percent of women and forty-three percent of men had been sexually harassed.[11] 17,700,0000 women had reported being sexually

---

[10] See https://www.nytimes.com/2017/06/30/technology/women-entrepreneurs-speak-out-sexual-harassment.html; https://www.nytimes.com/2017/07/03/technology/silicon-valley-sexual-harassment.html; https://www.theguardian.com/technology/2017/jul/09/silicon-valley-sexual-harassment-women-speak-up (Last visited 4/18/20).
[11] http://www.stopstreetharassment.org/wp-content/uploads/2018/01/Survey-Questions-2018-National-Study-on-Sexual-Harassment-and-Assault.pdf (last visited 4/20/20).

assaulted between the years of 1998 and 2017.[12]

Please think about that statistic for a moment. Let it sink in. Sexual assault has been illegal for centuries. Yet, so many women still experience it? Something must be wrong. Clearly, we must each take some responsibility for changing a society which allows such things to happen. Without a collective effort, these statistics won't change. Although the following chapters do not directly address sexual assault, reading them should help you understand what is and what is not illegal sexual harassment and give direction to your efforts to handle it correctly and productively in the workplace.

---

[12] Alanna Vagianos, 30 Alarming Statistics That Show The Reality Of Sexual Violence In America: This is what an epidemic looks like. Huffington Post, WOMEN 04/05/2017 12:09 pm ET Updated Apr 06, 2017 https://www.huffpost.com/entry/sexual-assault-statistics_n_58e24c14e4b0c777f788d24f (last visited 4/20/20).

Beth K. Whittenbury

CHAPTER 3

THE DIFFERENCE BETWEEN SEXUAL HARASSMENT AND SEXUAL ASSAULT

The media often confuses the terms "sexual harassment" and "sexual assault." However, to understand your rights and responsibilities in these areas, you need to understand the difference between the two. Sexual assault is a crime, as is rape. Sexual harassment is a civil action.

Rape has been a crime in some form since 1780 BC, when it was prohibited in The Code of Hammurabi, one of the first written laws. However, back then, since women were largely considered the property of a male, the Cod of Hammurabi defined the rape of a virgin as property damage to her father.[13] By the time of the American Colonies, rape was defined as a crime against the victim.[14] Sexual assault is also a crime against the victim. Sexual assault is defined as the unconsensual touching of another's intimate body part. Rape is

---

[13] Erika Eichelberger, Men Defining Rape: A History, *Mother Jones* POLITICS AUGUST 27, 2012 https://www.motherjones.com/politics/2012/08/men-defining-rape-history/ (last visited 4/20/20).

[14] Kyla Bishop, A Reflection on the History of Sexual Assault Laws in the United States, *The Arkansas Journal of Social Change and Public Service* April 15, 2018 https://ualr.edu/socialchange/2018/04/15/reflection-history-sexual-assault-laws-united-states/ (last visited 4/20/20).

unconsensual intercourse with someone. Therefore, the defense to a charge of rape or sexual assault is that the victim consented.

Criminal actions are brought in criminal court by a government employee, usually a member of a district attorney's office or attorney general's office. The victim does not bring the action to court. In a criminal proceeding, the victim appears in court as a witness.

The penalty for committing a crime is imprisonment or a fine, or both. If you are fined, you pay money. That money goes to the government, the party that brought the case to court, not to the victim. So, the victim's only role in a sexual assault case or a rape case is to state what happened on the witness stand and endure the cross examination of his or her testimony. As a reward for re-living, what could at best be traumatic memories, the victim receives no make-whole remedies other than perhaps seeing the perpetrator pay either financially to the government or with his or her freedom if sentenced to jail.

By contrast, sexual harassment is a civil action. In a civil action, the victim is called the plaintiff and he or she does bring the case to court, usually by hiring a lawyer to represent him or her. The case is heard in a different court system than the crimes of rape or sexual assault. Sexual harassment claims, as civil actions, are tried in civil court. Civil actions also allow the plaintiff - "the victim" - to recover monetary damages.

Although we will further define sexual harassment in the following chapter, the defense to sexual harassment is that the victim welcomed the behavior. You will note that the defense is different between the crimes of rape and sexual assault which use the defense of consent and sexual harassment which uses the defense that the acts were welcome. The difference between welcoming something and consenting to something can best be illustrated when we think about paying income tax. We generally consent to paying our taxes because we know we must or have no viable choice. However, few, if any of us, welcome paying those taxes.

So, in a case where a worker is told that she can keep her job if she sleeps with the boss, and she consents to do so in order to keep her job, she may not have a rape case, but she probably would have a sexual harassment case. She has consented to the act in order to keep her job, but not likely welcomed having to do so to in order to continue gainful employment.

Historically, unlike the crimes of rape and sexual assault, for which anyone could be found guilty, people could only sue their employers for sexual harassment. If you experienced unwelcome sexual conduct from someone who wasn't your employer, which didn't meet the definition of a crime, you didn't have a legal remedy. However, states have now begun to pass laws allowing victims to sue for sexual harassment which arises during the course of other types of relationships. Usually these relationships involve situations where the victim needs the help of someone in order to advance their rightful life activities, such as education, health care, or habitation. If such a service provider abuses the victim's dependence on the service provider, then the victim can sue for sexual harassment. California has such a law. California Civil Code Section 51.9 lists service providers such as a physician, psychotherapist, dentist, attorney, holder of a master's degree in social work, real estate agent, real estate appraiser, investor, accountant, banker, trust officer, financial planner loan officer, collection service, building contractor, or escrow loan officer, executor, trustee, or administrator, landlord or property manager, teacher, elected official, lobbyist, director or producer as some examples of those, other than employers, who can be sued for sexual harassment in California.

Beth K. Whittenbury

CHAPTER 4

WHAT IS SEXUAL HARASSMENT?

Sexual harassment is a difficult concept for some people, because behavior that is perfectly acceptable to one person may constitute harassment to someone else. For example, a YouGov poll showed that more women than men say that asking someone out, making sexual jokes, and other sexual behaviors at work constitute sexual harassment. Specifically, forty-nine percent of men said they thought asking for sexual favors at work is "always" sexual harassment, compared to seventy-one percent of women. Sixty-six percent of women feel sexually harassed when people look at their "private parts" at work, while only forty percent of men feel the same way.[15]

  According to the law, a person's motive for behaving a certain way is not a factor in determining whether behavior constitutes sexual harassment. Supervisors must remember that there is no "innocent

---

[15] Statistics quoted from "Do you need verbal consent for holding hands, kissing, sex? The differences between men and women may surprise you" By Erica Evans @Erica_Lee_Evans Nov 27, 2018, 10:00pm MST *Deseret News* found at https://www.deseret.com/2018/11/28/20659580/do-you-need-verbal-consent-for-holding-hands-kissing-sex-the-differences-between-men-and-women-may-s#parker-wilson-opens-the-door-for-paige-eastwood-during-a-dinner-date-at-mo-bettahs-in-lehi-on-thursday-nov-15-2018 (last visited 4/21/20).

until proven guilty" standard for workplace sexual harassment cases. The credibility of the parties must be weighed in determining if alleged behaviors did or did not occur. Also, many people may feel "harassed," but the behavior they fault may not qualify as sexual harassment under the legal standards defined by the courts, legislature, or regulatory agencies. For example, constantly calling someone out for being late to work or missing deadlines does not constitute illegal harassment, unless the company is using different standards of compliance for different genders or different groups protected from discrimination by law. Supervisors should indiscriminately address all behaviors that impact employee productivity and attendance in the workplace.

At its core, sexual harassment is a form of sex discrimination prohibited in employment situations by Title VII of the Civil Rights Act of 1964. You should remember that sexual harassment is wrong because it hinders the ability of one gender to advance their career as easily as another. Although some people push back against the theory of sexual harassment, most of us agree that everyone should have a fair and level playing field for advancement. Our hard work, talent, and skill should determine our success, not characteristics such as gender or race over which we have no control.

Although the Civil Rights Act was originally passed to prohibit racial discrimination, the law also prohibits discrimination based on national origin, color, creed, religion, and gender. In addition, federal laws prohibit discrimination based on age, genetic information, and disability (including taking time off under the Family and Medical Care Leave Act (FMLA)), while some states, such as California, add additional categories such as marital status, gender preference and gender expression to those protected from discrimination. So, although this book focuses on sexual harassment, remember that much of the analysis described also applies to the other types of harassment prohibited by law.

The Equal Opportunity Employment Commission ("EEOC"), the federal agency tasked with the enforcement of Title VII of the Civil Rights Act of 1964, defines sexual harassment as:

Unwelcome sexual advances, requests for sexual favors, and other verbal or physical conduct of a sexual nature when this conduct explicitly or implicitly affects an individual's employment, unreasonably interferes with an individual's work performance, or creates an intimidating, hostile, or offensive work environment.[16]

The concept of sexual harassment has further developed through court cases. **Now there are essentially two kinds of sexual harassment: 1) Hostile Environment; and 2) Quid Pro Quo.**

The EEOC definition of sexual harassment can seem a bit cumbersome and difficult to apply to everyday experiences or factual situations. In addition, sexual harassment situations are often emotionally charged. So, to determine if you are dealing with one of these types of sexual harassment, you may find it helpful to think about the facts in terms of a straightforward formula. For example, if A, B, and C are all present then, together, they equal sexual harassment. Then all we need to know is what do the A, B and C stand for in the formula.

Generic Formula: $A+B+C$ = Sexual Harassment

Then we can further apply the formula to each type of sexual harassment.

Formula for Hostile Environment:

For hostile environment harassment, A = unwelcome; B = sexual conduct; and C = the unwelcome sexual conduct has become so severe or pervasive that it has created a hostile or offensive working

---

[16] https://www.eeoc.gov/eeoc/publications/fs-sex.cfm (last visited 4/21/2020).

environment. Thus, the formula is:

A (Unwelcome) + B (Sexual conduct) + C (So severe or pervasive that it has created a hostile or offensive working environment) = Hostile Environment Sexual Harassment

Formula for Quid Pro Quo (Tangible Employment Action) sexual harassment:

Quid pro quo is a Latin term meaning, essentially, this for that. The phrase stands for an exchange of benefits. The original United States Supreme Court case to establish a claim for sexual harassment used the term "quid pro quo" to identify one type of sexual harassment case plaintiffs can bring to court. More recent US Supreme Court decisions speak in terms of "tangible employment actions." Both terms describe the same type of case.

We also have a formula for quid pro quo sexual harassment. Here we find that the first two elements, the A and the B, if you will, are the same as in hostile environment cases. So the third element, or "C," within the equation distinguishes quid pro quo from hostile environment cases. Please note that in either case, **you need all three elements (A, B, and C) before you have an actionable, legal claim for either kind of sexual harassment.**

For quid pro quo claims, the A still equals unwelcome, the B still equals sexual conduct, but now the C stands for an employment decision based on the victim's acquiescence to the unwelcome sexual behavior. Thus, the formula for quid pro quo sexual harassment is:

A (Unwelcome) + B (Sexual conduct) + C (An employment decision based on the victim's acquiescence to the unwelcome sexual behavior) = Quid Pro Quo Harassment

Now, let's define each of those three terms in the equations.

Unwelcome

Behavior may be unwelcome even if we intend it kindly. Again, the motive of the perpetrator does not matter in sexual harassment cases. The relevant fact is how the recipient felt about the behavior. Individuals **do not** have to tell the perpetrator that he or she finds the behavior offensive or unwelcome. It is enough if they do not return the behavior, do not laugh at the jokes, make a face, turn away, or start avoiding the offender. In other words, body language counts. However, even if no one sees any outward indication that the behavior is unwelcome, it just has to **be** unwelcome to meet this part of the test. In other words, the "A" element of the equation is completely subjective on the part of the person complaining. However, remember that according to our equation, unwelcome is only one of three things you need to find before there is an actionable, legal case of sexual harassment.

In some cases it may seem that the person complaining is "too sensitive." However, **do not** substitute your judgment for theirs. Frankly, for this part of the analysis, what you think about the behavior is irrelevant. All that you need to determine is whether the person now raising the objection genuinely felt that the behavior was unwelcome.

You will find cases where the person complaining engages in the exact same behavior s/he is complaining about with other people, but with this one person, s/he finds it offensive. Under the law, people have the right to deny certain conduct from some people while accepting that same conduct from others with whom they have closer relationships. For example, a woman might tell dirty jokes with a male colleague she has known for a long time, but files a sexual harassment complaint when the new guy tries to tell her some off-color jokes. That claim can be valid. The courts are split over whether other actions of the plaintiff need to be taken into account. Whether the person complaining should clearly convey that the conduct is unwelcome from one person when s/he accepts it from another will depend on the courts in your jurisdiction. So err on the side of safety and do not require the victim to make clear that certain behavior is unwelcome.

Supervisors can convey this message for subordinates, and subordinates may ask them to do so. A current trend now, called bystander training, also encourages co-workers to speak up for each other. So, if you think a fellow employee looks uncomfortable or you see inappropriate behavior, feel free to say something for the benefit of the workforce.

In quid pro quo cases, we often find that what one party thought was a "welcome" affair later turns into a sexual harassment claim. Although there may not have been any outward indication during the affair that such a relationship was unwelcome, there is nothing to keep a subordinate employee from later stating that s/he only went along with the behavior because it seemed necessary to keep a job. This outcome shows why, even in states with constitutional privacy provisions, a supervisor should view dating subordinates as an extremely risky practice. The same problem can occur even when peers date each other. If one party has better connections with higher decision makers within the organization, the other can again claim that s/he only went along with the affair in order to better secure his or her position within the company.

If you become aware of a sexual relationship between two employees, know that the moment repercussions of the relationship trickle into the workplace, it becomes the company's business. Although in California and some other states, state constitutional privacy constraints prohibit employers from telling employees they cannot date each other during their off hours, the moment that dating causes work-related issues, the employer needs to and has the right to address it.

As a supervisor, you may find yourself in the position of needing to ask employees if they truly welcome the relationships of which you've become aware. If they tell you that they do, make a note of that fact, including the date and time you had the discussion. Place that note in a confidential file to which only you have access. Should the allegation arise that you knew of the affair and took no steps to protect the employee, you can then prove that you upheld your managerial duties by asking the question and acting accordingly.

If an employee tells you s/he does not completely welcome the affair but feels compelled to continue, take steps to help that employee get out of the relationship with no adverse job consequences. In such a case, you should consult your human resources manager or the company's general counsel. Do not try to determine the steps to take by yourself. Just know that you have the obligation to seek expert help within the company about exactly what to do and that you must do something. You cannot turn a blind eye because you are uncomfortable with the situation or unsure of the best course of action.

Note that welcoming behavior is different than consenting to behavior. As stated previously, the standard in rape cases is consent - did the person consent to have sexual relations? However, in sexual harassment cases, we use "unwelcome" as the standard. A person can consent to conduct that he or she does not welcome. For example, you can stay and listen to a dirty joke rather than making a scene by leaving. Simply remaining to hear the joke does not mean that the person wanted to hear it or welcomed having to listen to it. One cannot always easily leave a situation in the workplace. You need to stay there to get the job done whether you like what's going on around you or not.

Often, people don't like to complain even about offensive conduct. They don't want to look like a prude or a whiner. So supervisors should diligently watch what goes on in the workplace. If you see something unnecessary to the work at hand that might be considered offensive, stop it. Don't wait until someone has endured enough unwelcome conduct that s/he is ready to file a lawsuit to get it to stop. Supervisors can hope that employees will let management know their feelings before taking such a step. However, in reality, most people will think that if members of management see the behavior but do nothing about it, it would be pointless to file a complaint or bring their concerns to management. So managers need to be proactive to set the right tone for the organization and set the standard that illegal harassment is not tolerated.

Sexual Conduct

The sexual conduct element of our equation is an objective one. Would reasonable people agree that the scenario includes an element of sexual conduct? The courts have interpreted the sexual conduct part of the sexual harassment test to include not only conduct that is about sex, but also conduct that differentiates between genders. Remember that sexual harassment is illegal because it is a form of employment discrimination prohibited by Title VII of the Civil Rights Act of 1964. Therefore, if an employee treats men and women differently on the job, that differential treatment constitutes sexual conduct for the purpose of our analysis. Sexual conduct can also occur between members of the same gender, so don't just look for male/female scenarios. Courts have upheld cases were men have sexually harassed other men and women have sexually harassed other women.

In reality, courts don't always articulate the gender distinction in their opinions. Often, they seem to feel that where conduct is about sex, there must be a gender distinction in the facts somewhere. For example, this male boss wouldn't be propositioning his secretary if she wasn't female. However, in same-sex cases, the courts more consistently state the gender distinction. It is possible for females or males to be biased against their own gender. For example, a female boss may consistently make disparaging remarks about other women in the workplace, but never the men. In cases like these you may not find anything that you would consider "sexual" going on. Still, a gender distinction is being made and can give rise to liability.

Clearly, where the conduct does include sexual elements, the company may face liability. Consequently, conduct or speech that is about sex should be limited or removed from the workplace. Even if **you** don't feel that such conduct is offensive, it may be offensive to others.[17] Remember workers can't leave the area without impacting their job performance and, consequently, their livelihood. What does

---

[17] See Appendix A for a list of actions which may constitute sexual conduct.

this mean in a practical sense? Management should remove all posters or calendars of scantily-clad people from the workplace. Watch for inappropriate e-mails, screen savers, or memes and report those to IT or management for follow up and removal. Report offensive computer spam to the IT department. It is the company's duty to keep the workplace free from sexually offensive material or actions, whether they come from internal employees or external sources such as vendors, clients or computer spam.

Businesses should not allow dirty jokes. Truly funny jokes, which do not put down a protected category of people, shouldn't create a problem. We don't have to remove fun from the workplace, just harmful or offensive conduct. There are ways to have fun without offending anyone. Set a good example yourself. Supervisors should be available for and responsive to any complaints. Treat all your fellow employees with respect.

If you see or overhear conduct that you think might have offended someone, pull the potentially offended employee aside later and gently inquire as to how s/he received the comment or conduct. Even if employees express no concerns, remind them that you and the company are committed to providing a harmonious working environment. Supervisors taking those steps should document their discussions and any follow up in confidential files which include dates and the employee responses. This will help protect supervisors later by showing that they acted proactively to uphold company policy. Supervisors should also let the company Human Resources (HR) manager know about the conversations so that if another manager does so as well, HR can begin to see a pattern that the company may have to address. Supervisors should constantly remind employees that the company has anti-harassment policies and that management is an open, committed conduit for complaints.

If you view conduct or speech that is potentially harassing, also pull aside the perpetrator and explain that the conduct wasn't of the highest professional standard and that you know s/he can do better. If you think the conduct was acceptable, but might be misconstrued, convey that message as well. Don't wait for complaints to come. We can all be proactive in creating a harmonious environment.

Severe or Pervasive

When does sexual conduct become so severe or pervasive that it alters the original conditions of employment and creates a hostile working environment? That is a tough question to answer, because in most cases there are no clear lines. However, the EEOC has said that one harmful offensive touching of an intimate body area immediately creates a hostile environment. Other than that circumstance, lawyers and juries need to use their judgment as to when the line has been crossed. Being thrown against the wall and molested at work just one time would probably make most people feel that the workplace has become a hostile environment. They wouldn't want to return or endure the behavior again. However, one dirty joke heard over the course of a ten-year tenure with the company would probably not constitute a hostile environment for most people.

This element of sexual harassment claims is both an objective and a subjective one. First the person complaining must feel their work environment is hostile or abusive. However, the plaintiff's personal feelings, although one thing they need to prove at trial, are not enough to establish the severe or pervasive element of a hostile environment sexual harassment case. Under the law, there is also a reasonable person standard that applies when deciding if behavior is severe or pervasive enough to create a hostile working environment. Ask yourself, "Would a reasonable person of the same gender and in the same circumstances as the person complaining find this behavior offensive?" Granted, this is not a perfect standard. Even within the same gender, people vary greatly in their comfort levels with certain types of behaviors. Try to find a middle ground and apply that standard. The "reasonable" standard has been applied in negligence cases by the courts for over a hundred years and appears to be the best we can do in our justice system, so do the best you can with it. Remember too, that in addition to what a reasonable person would think, the plaintiff him or herself must also have felt they were forced to work in a hostile environment.

The good news is that individual supervisors don't need to make that call. As stated before, supervisors and to an extent rank and file employees should be proactive. If you see or hear of inappropriate conduct, address it immediately. Don't allow repeated offenses. Management shouldn't wait until offensive conduct has happened so many times that the offended employee hires a lawyer and files a lawsuit.

How management ends offensive behavior will vary with the conduct in question. It is not always necessary to fire the offender, but in some cases, like grabbing an intimate body part, companies may decide to immediately terminate the offender. Some cases require only a serious discussion and warning. However, case law demonstrates that where a serious discussion and warning does not stop the conduct, more severe discipline is required to show that the company is taking appropriate action. The bottom-line obligation is to stop the conduct immediately, whatever it takes. A complainant should not have to make more than one complaint to resolve the situation. So employers should do what they must to get the message across the first time. Again, most employers have a human resources expert on staff with whom supervisors should consult to decide which steps would be most appropriate in any given case.

Although the company's obligation is to stop any behavior leading to hostile environments, there are still things employees can do at work to have fun without offending anyone. Strive for a fun and harmonious environment where everyone is respectful and professional, but not too tense. One pat on the shoulder is not sexual harassment. Neither is a true, straight-forward compliment. However, a compliment accompanied by a once-over could be sexual harassment. We all know when "compliments" are a pretext for a come-on. So, don't overreact, but do keep an eye on how the compliments, jokes, or touching is received. Remember, body language speaks volumes. So if the shoulder patting is constant and the receiving employee always pulls away, you should speak to the shoulder patter and explain that they should probably refrain in the future. However, if two employees start the day with a mutual back pat, and s/he are both smiling, that's probably a sign that the situation is not offensive to either party.

When you genuinely compliment someone you're trying to make that person happy or feel good about themselves. If their body language expresses the opposite reaction, make a note to yourself that your statement did not have the desired effect, and refrain from making such comments to that person again. Don't take offense at their reaction. Just note it and respond appropriately. We all have different comfort levels. When you determine a co-workers comfort level, respect it. In that way, we can build harmonious workplaces for all.

Often employees and even supervisors mistakenly feel that company policy does not apply to company events that are held off company property, such as corporate retreats or extended training sessions. A work-sponsored event is still work and all the same rules apply. Just because alcohol is flowing or you're dressed in jeans, you can't suddenly act unprofessionally.

As a manager, set a good example at all times and make sure that your employees follow your example. Employees can't unsee behavior. Therefore, if you find yourself at a bar on your own time, and not a company event, but a subordinate enters, your behavior there will reflect on your effectiveness in the workplace. So comport yourself professionally or change bar venues to one with no co-workers present.

Remember too, that even if you do a legal analysis and decide that the alleged harassment does not constitute a sexual harassment claim, someone **felt** harassed or they would not have complained in the first place. Statistics show that most claims of harassment are not made up. In fact, many more people experience harassment than actually have the courage to complain. So if an employee complains, something should be done to alleviate the problem. Maybe a manager needs to undergo some interpersonal skills training. Maybe employees are not treating each other with the proper respect. Don't ignore a complaint just because it does not constitute a legal claim. Where disharmony exists, everyone is less productive. See what can be done to alleviate the situation and rejuvenate employees.

An Employment Decision was Based on Acquiescence

An employment decision based on acquiescence to unwelcome sexual conduct is the third element of a quid pro quo or tangible employment action claim. "Quid pro quo" is Latin for "this for that." So, in order to have a claim for quid pro quo sexual harassment, something must be traded between the parties. The boss might say, "Sleep with me tonight and I'll give you a promotion in the morning." However, instead of using a carrot, the boss might use a stick such as, "If you don't sleep with me tonight, then I'll fire you in the morning."

Real life situations are rarely this straightforward. Sometimes a supervisor enters into a sexual relationship with a subordinate thinking the subordinate welcomes the relationship. However, let's say things don't work out, and the sexual relationship ends. Tensions associated with the breakup spill over into the work environment. The subordinate's next raise isn't as high as his or her last one. S/he makes a claim of quid pro quo harassment. How would a supervisor defend him or herself?

Suppose the subordinate says that s/he never welcomed the relationship and felt s/he needed to acquiesce in order to stay employed. How do you defend yourself against that statement? Remember there is no "innocent until proven guilty" standard in sexual harassment cases. If the employer investigates such a claim, the investigator will need to assess the credibility of the parties. If all activity and conversation took place behind closed doors, then the supervisor will have a hard time justifying his or her past actions. Let's face it, a relationship between a supervisor and subordinate is fraught with peril. The supervisor is putting his or her job on the line.

Employment decisions can include anything to which there

might be a reference in the employee's personnel file. These actions might include hiring, firing, shift assignments, promotions, demotions, job changes, discipline, and excessive absenteeism or tardiness. If you start documenting any employee, make sure that you document them only to the extent you do all your other subordinates. Treating anyone differently is a form of discrimination, and sexual harassment is a discrimination claim. If you treat someone differently you have to be able to prove that there is a legitimate and legal reason for the differential treatment.

Often managers will make decisions quickly without thinking them through. These days we are all pressured to make instant decisions. Maybe it just feels like the right time to change everyone's shift assignment or reassign secretaries. Be careful that you can articulate a legitimate business reason for those decisions. Perhaps you don't know about the declined advance some other manager made to one of the secretaries, and then, the next day, you arbitrarily reassign that secretary. The secretary may assume it's a message that he or she shouldn't have rebuffed the advance. How do you prove that your decision wasn't in response to what went on with the other manager? You should have written documentation describing the legitimate reason for the reassignment, such as a seniority system or that the reassignment was part of established rotation system followed throughout the department and set up well in advance.

Federal law often now speaks in terms of a tangible employment action instead of quid pro quo. They are really talking about the same thing. However, we should know what the federal enforcement agency has to say on the subject.

The EEOC Questions and Answers for Small Employers on Employer Liability for Harassment by Supervisors says, "An employer is always responsible for harassment by a supervisor that culminated in a tangible employment action." The EEOC defines "tangible employment action" as a "significant change in employment status." In its enforcement guidance, the EEOC states that a tangible employment action is the means by which a supervisor wields the official power of the company over subordinates. When used as a method of illegal harassment, it usually inflicts direct economic harm to the victim employee.

An action qualifies as "tangible" if it results in a significant change of employment status. For example, significantly changing an employee's duties is a tangible employment action even if the employee maintains the same salary and benefits. Altering an employee's duties in a way that decreases his or her chance for promotion or salary increases is also a tangible job detriment.

It doesn't matter if employees acquiesce to unwelcome, sexual conduct, or if they spurn it. Employees can sue for quid pro quo even if they received a promotion because they put up with the unwelcome conduct. The United States Supreme Court has stated that it is enough that there be a significant *change* in employment status. The Court does not require that the change be detrimental to qualify as tangible.

Questions often arise as to whether a threat of an employment action constitutes a quid pro quo claim or whether the supervisor needs to actually follow through on a threat before a legitimate quid pro quo claim arises. The United States Supreme Court has clarified that quid pro quo claims require an actual employment decision and that cases involving threats of employment decisions should be analyzed as hostile environment cases. In other words, are the threats severe or pervasive enough to create a hostile environment?

Test Your Knowledge

The following vignettes allow you to see if you've understood and can apply the concepts we've covered so far. Take the time to read and think about them before looking for the answers and explanations in Appendix C.

1. Sally is a lower-level manager in a corporation. The head of her department makes disparaging remarks about females at least once a day. This manager says that women are dumb, that they work slower than men, that they are

not as fun to work with as men and that they always mess up the company softball team because they can't play as well as the men. Once, when Sally was in the middle of a big presentation to important clients, and the projector stopped working, the department head said, "Well, what do you expect from a woman?"

Is this a case of sexual harassment and if so, what kind of sexual harassment claim would Sally file?

2. Robert often tells dirty jokes to his friend and co-worker Al, who always responds with a good humored laugh. Fresia sits next to Al and sometimes overhears these jokes. After a while, Fresia starts to tell Al a dirty joke every time she comes to her desk in the morning. Al finds these jokes offensive coming from Fresia and politely asks her to knock it off. Fresia responds, "Hey, I know you like those kinds of jokes, because you laugh when Robert tells them."

As a supervisor, you overhear this interchange between Al and Fresia. What should you do?

3. Two doctors at a hospital engage in a sexual relationship during their off hours away from the hospital. One doctor is a former Chief of Staff and the other is relatively new to the hospital. Neither doctor reports to the other in an official capacity. After a few months, the relationship ends. The next month, the hospital board tells the doctor newest to the hospital that her services are no longer needed and terminates her employment.

Does she have a sexual harassment claim? If so, which kind and under what circumstances?

CHAPTER 5

RETALIATION: THE OTHER LEGAL CLAIM ASSOCIATED WITH HARASSMENT/DISCRIMINATION

In addition to quid pro quo and hostile environment claims, employees or former employees may sometimes claim that a company, its supervisors or employees retaliated against him or her for making a sexual harassment complaint. Retaliation claims are becoming more prevalent in the courts. The law which makes retaliation of this kind illegal is the same law that prohibits employment discrimination – Title VII of the Civil Rights Act of 1964.

To establish a retaliation claim, the plaintiff must first show that he or she engaged in some sort of "protected activity." In other words, the plaintiff engaged in an activity legally protected from retaliation. Making a claim of sexual harassment within an organization is a legally protected activity, as is supporting or refuting such a claim during an ensuing investigation. Some courts construe "protected activity" quite broadly to include anything you might do to uphold or act in accordance with discrimination laws. One circuit court even allowed a plaintiff to meet the protected activity prong by engaging in activity that wasn't actually protected under law, because the court reasoned that she and most reasonable people would think that her activity was protected under anti-discrimination laws.

After establishing that he or she engaged in a protected activity, the plaintiff must show that he or she was subjected to an "adverse action" because of the protected activity. On this point, courts tell us that the proper inquiry is whether the employer's action "well might have dissuaded a reasonable worker from making or supporting a charge of discrimination."[18] Although the term "adverse action" sounds equivalent to an "employment decision," an adverse action allows for a much broader category of actions than just employment decisions. Finally, the plaintiff needs to show a causal link between the protected activity and the adverse action. In other words, but for filing a sexual harassment claim, the employer would not have taken the adverse action against the employee.

So carefully watch the actions you take with respect to employees who have been involved with a sexual harassment complaint. Reassignment of duties has been found to be retaliatory even where the former and present duties fell within the same job description. So has suspension without pay even when the employee was later reinstated with back pay.

Co-worker treatment of someone who has filed a claim may also give rise to retaliation claims. Therefore, employers should watch, not only the response of management to the person filing the claim, but also the responses of that person's co-workers. Unchecked rumors about or a sudden lack of co-worker socializing with an employee who has filed a complaint may qualify as retaliation. Supervisors must do all in their power to protect those within the organization who exercise their rights under company policy from any actions which could reasonably be construed as retaliatory.

To use our formula approach for retaliation, you can apply the following to any fact pattern to determine if all the required elements of a retaliation claim are present:

---

[18] Burlington N. & S.F. Ry. Co. v. White, 548 U.S. 53, 65 (2006).

Retaliation Formula: A (An employee engaged in protected activity) + B (The employer took adverse action) + C (But for the employee engaging in the protected activity, the employer would not have taken the adverse action) = Retaliation

Test Your Knowledge

Please try to reason through this vignette yourself before checking the answer guide found in Appendix C.

4. Ally was recently named "Regional Manager of the Year" by her cosmetics company employer. One day, she and her boss, the Regional VP, walked through one of the department stores at which the company leased a cosmetics counter. When the VP saw the woman behind the counter, he told Ally to fire the worker and replace her with someone "hot" like the voluptuous blond he pointed to in a neighboring department. Ally was taken aback, but didn't respond and didn't fire the counter employee. Later, the VP asked Ally again to fire the employee. Ally did not refuse. She did not file a complaint with HR. She simply asked for a reasonable justification for the firing to which the VP replied that he didn't have to give her one. Ally did not fire the counter employee. Shortly thereafter, the VP started auditing Ally's expense reports and asking her subordinates to tell him anything Ally had ever done wrong. Ally began receiving below-average performance evaluations and was eventually put on probation. She went out on stress leave and ultimately quit, claiming constructive discharge and retaliation.[19]

Does Ally have a retaliation case?

---

[19] These facts are based on those from an actual case: Yanowitz v. L'Oreal, 116 P.2d 1123 (Cal. 2005).

5. Two male employees filed a sexual harassment claim. Their employer hired a private investigator, ostensibly to investigate the claim. Instead, he undertook an invasive background check on the two employees who filed the claim. The P.I. asked their friends and co-workers embarrassing and awkward questions about the two men. When the employer discovered this, it fired the investigator and retained outside counsel who then investigated the harassment claims. The two employees sued for retaliation.[20]

Do the two employees have a retaliation case?

---

[20] These facts are based on those from an actual case: EEOC v. Video Only, Inc., No. 06-1362-KI, 2008 U.S. Dist. LEXIS 46094 (D. Or. June 11, 2008).

CHAPTER 6

COMPANY LIABILITY

Company Liability for Sexual Harassment Done By Supervisors

The standards for company liability for acts of a supervisor vary between federal and state jurisdictions. Most jurisdictions agree that if a supervisor engages in quid pro quo sexual harassment, the company will be liable even if it does not condone the behavior and has written policies against such behavior. This outcome stems from the doctrine of Respondeat Superior which the United States adopted from English common law.

"Respondeat Superior" basically means, "let the master answer." Remember that back in jolly ole England, the Lord of the Manor, the master, had servants he would send on errands. If, while on an errand for the master, the servant injured a peasant, the peasant could not get a remedy from a servant who worked primarily for room and board. In order to fashion a fair result in such cases, the courts decided to hold the master accountable for the actions of his servants while they were about their master's business.

We don't like to think of ourselves as servants, but the employer/employee relationship essentially mirrors that of master and servant. The employer still, generally, has deeper pockets than the employee. So, if an employee, especially a manager or supervisor who is acting for the employer as management, makes an employment decision for a discriminatory reason, that illegal behavior is attributed to the employer. Thus, the employer is automatically liable, even if it has a policy against that type of behavior. If the employer had not given the supervisor the authority to make employment decision on behalf of the employer, the injury – the illegal harassment or discrimination – would not have occurred.

Therefore, we can understand why the company is held strictly or automatically liable for quid pro quo sexual harassment, which requires an employment action as one of its elements. What about cases of hostile environment perpetrated by supervisors? Again, the answer differs between states and the federal jurisdictions. If a supervisor in California, for example, engages in or allows behavior that constitutes a hostile environment, the company remains liable but may try to reduce the damages for which it is deemed responsible. To do so in California, the employer will use a judicially-created tactic known as the "Avoidable Consequences Doctrine."

Under that doctrine, the damages a complainant can recover in a court case are limited to the damages that the complainant would have suffered if s/he had used the company's internal reporting procedures to address the problem in-house. In other words, an employer is not liable for damages that an employee could have avoided with reasonable effort and without undue risk, expense, or humiliation.

Federal law takes a slightly different approach in cases where supervisors have engaged in hostile environment harassment. Under federal law, employers may raise an affirmative defense in cases where a supervisor engaged in sexual harassment but took no tangible employment action against the employee. Successful application of this affirmative defense removes all liability from the employer. Although the affirmative defense is an absolute defense under federal law which completely exonerates employers where it applies, the elements necessary to establish the federal affirmative defense are essentially equivalent to the elements of the Avoidable Consequences Doctrine.

The Avoidable Consequences Doctrine has three elements: 1) the employer took reasonable steps to prevent and correct workplace sexual harassment; 2) the employee unreasonably failed to use the preventive and corrective measures that the employer provided; and 3) reasonable use of the employer's procedures would have prevented at least some of the harm that the employee suffered. The federal affirmative defense has two elements: 1) the employer exercised reasonable care to prevent and promptly correct any harassing behavior; and 2) the employee unreasonably failed to take advantage of any preventive or corrective opportunities provided by the employer or to otherwise avoid harm.[21] You'll note that the two definitions appear similar.

One of the first things a court will look at to determine whether an employer took reasonable steps to prevent or correct workplace sexual harassment is the company's sexual harassment policy. A good policy will include: 1) a statement that sexual harassment is illegal; 2) the legal definition of sexual harassment; 3) a statement that sexual harassment is against company policy; 4) examples of behaviors which can qualify as sexual harassment; 5) a complaint procedure with multiple avenues of complaint; 6) a statement that any complaints will be handled as confidentially as possible; 7) a statement prohibiting retaliation against anyone bringing a claim or participating in the investigation of a claim; 8) the remedies available for sexual harassment; 9) the possible consequences to those found guilty of sexual harassment; and 10) how and where to report sexual harassment. Please review your company's policy and familiarize yourself with your company's complaint procedure.

Just having a policy against sexual harassment with these ten elements included is not enough. The policy must be implemented

---

[21] June 18, 1999 EEOC Enforcement Guidance on Vicarious Employer Liability for Unlawful Harassment by Supervisors, https://www.eeoc.gov/laws/guidance/enforcement-guidance-vicarious-liability-unlawful-harassment-supervisors (Last visited 5/8/2020).

and proven effective within your organization. You can't have a policy, but not enforce it, and still apply the Avoidable Consequences Doctrine or federal affirmative defense. If a plaintiff can successfully argue that there was no point in following the company procedures because the company was not committed to upholding its policies, then the Avoidable Consequences Doctrine or affirmative defense will not apply.

What Does All This Mean to Supervisors?

Basically, supervisors are responsible for implementing company procedures so a member of management must know, understand and apply the company policies against harassment in the workplace. If you receive a complaint, take it seriously and follow the procedures provided. If there are no procedures provided, you must still take steps to determine whether a remedy is appropriate and if so, apply the appropriate remedy. When in doubt, contact the Human Resources Department for guidance immediately.

Keep the claim as confidential as possible. Avoid any appearance of retaliation in response to the claim. Squelch rumors where possible. You want to be able to show that you created an atmosphere that encourages employees to come forward with complaints. Maintain an open door policy. Respond effectively to any complaints you receive. If a case ultimately goes to trial, you want the jury to find that you and the company did all that you could reasonably have done to prevent and correct the situation.

Who is a Supervisor?

Since we just discussed that in some cases, an employer can be held strictly liable for the actions of their supervisor, we need a working understanding of who constitutes a supervisor within a company. Again federal law differs from state laws in determining who is a supervisor. Under federal discrimination law, a supervisor is one who has company bestowed authority to take tangible employment actions against the complainant.[22]

State laws differ in how they define a supervisor in sexual harassment cases. In California, an individual qualifies as a supervisor if:

A) the individual has authority to undertake or recommend tangible employment decisions affecting the employee; or

B) the individual has authority to direct the employee's daily work activities; or

C) anyone who can resolve employee grievances or recommend such action by exercising independent judgment; or

D) the individual has apparent authority to do A, B or C.

Therefore, if you have co-workers making shift assignments, they might be considered supervisors. Also, if you have a peer review process, it is possible that those peer reviews could be construed as recommendations for employment decisions and thus qualify all those peers as supervisors for the purposes of assessing liability. Therefore, in states like California, employers should carefully choose to whom they give the power to influence or make employment decisions.

For the purposes of determining liability, any person with the apparent authority to do the above two things will also constitute a supervisor in states such as California. Apparent authority means that, although the person doesn't actually have the authority to act as a supervisor, other employees reasonably believe that they do. If so, then the company is bound by the actions of those they have not made clear lack company authority for those actions. For example, in some organizations, the lines of command become blurred and employees may not clearly know who really has the power to direct their work. Make sure the lines of command are clearly known within your organization, and if you see or hear of someone overreaching their

---

[22] Vance v. Ball State University, 570 U.S. 421 (2013).

bounds, stop him or her immediately.

Company Liability for Sexual Harassment Done By Coworkers

In California and at the federal level, the employer is not strictly liable for the actions of the rank and file who are below the level of supervisor. The employer is liable for a hostile environment created by co-workers only if it knew or reasonably should have known of the hostile environment and failed to take immediate steps to end the harassment. Therefore, if a supervisor sees co-workers harassing each other or creating a hostile work environment, and s/he does nothing, the company will be liable for hostile environment sexual harassment. So, supervisors cannot turn a blind eye to potentially harassing behavior. Management shouldn't wait for a complaint. Employers must be proactive in handling inappropriate behavior in the workplace.

However, if the harassment takes place behind closed doors, then it is likely that the company will not know about it until someone in the organization complains. Once management receives a complaint, the manager and the company must immediately act to determine whether the complaint is valid.[23] If an unbiased investigation concludes that illegal harassment occurred, the organization must remedy the harassment. See the section below entitled: "Tools for Managers" for a thorough discussion of how to receive complaints.

---

[23] Generally, the way to determine if a complaint is valid is to conduct an investigation. To learn more about conducting investigations please see my book, *Investigating the Workplace Harassment Claim*, published by the American Bar Association and available through Amazon.com or at www.ShopABA.org.

CHAPTER 7

STEPS TO TAKE IF YOU EXPERIENCE SEXUAL HARASSMENT WITHIN THE WORKPLACE

Preparing to Bring a Complaint

If you are unsure whether you're experiencing actionable sexual harassment, review the chapter entitled, "What is Sexual Harassment?," and run your situation through the A+B+C test explained in chapter four. If your analysis indicates that you are suffering from illegal conduct, next check your company's policy on sexual harassment. The policy should lay out the company's complaint procedure. Typically, the policy will give you several options of people within the company authorized to receive your complaint. Give some thought to which of these will most likely hear your concerns in a neutral manner and take the responsibility for seeing the complaint procedures through.

Before meeting with that person, do your best to document and gather any evidence you may have that will help the employer see the validity of your claim. Do, you have texts or emails that show the harassment? Did you take any pictures of the offensive behavior? Who witnessed the incidents? Who did you tell about the incidents shortly after they happened? If you can go in prepared to calmly present supporting evidence of your claim, that will make the process easier for everyone. Get a hold of your emotions so that you can present your concerns in a calm and professional manner. Bring the company's sexual harassment policy and complaint procedure with you to reference if you feel the need to back up your decision to come forward.

You may be asked to repeat your story to Human Resources, so be prepared to do so. Some employers may ask you to put your complaint in writing. If so, you should comply. Refrain from informing the general workplace about your claims until the company has had a chance to confirm them in as confidential a manner as possible. If news of your claim gets back to the alleged harasser before the company can speak with him or her, that can impact the company's ability to get a clear picture of the facts. Ultimately, you will probably be asked to participate in an investigation.

The Investigation Process

Unless whoever will form the ultimate conclusion about the truthfulness of a sexual harassment allegation actually witnessed the alleged event or behavior, the company must conduct a timely, unbiased, and thorough investigation of the employee's complaint. The purpose of the investigation is to determine the facts of the case. An impartial fact-finder from within or without the company should conduct the investigation. Usually, the complainant, accused, and all relevant witnesses will be interviewed. The fact-finder will likely interview whoever initially received the complaint as well. The fact-finder may not interview every witness identified by the accused and complainant, but should interview enough people to form clear factual conclusions as to each of the allegations.

The investigation may take a while. During that process, complainants should be kept safe from any further harassment and not experience any retaliation for having submitted a claim. You may find the accused placed on leave or you may be allowed to work from home. How the company will handle those issues will depend on the facts of the case. However the employer handles this period, your career should not receive any negative impact, even temporarily, in response to your filing a sexual harassment complaint. A company representative should keep you apprised of the progress of the investigation and give periodic updates on the expected time to completion of the investigation. However, understand that employers may not have firm answers to those questions. Investigations can sometimes take far longer than initially anticipated. Relevant witnesses may be on leave or otherwise difficult to locate. So, try to exhibit patience. As long as management keeps you apprised of the progress, and you can continue your work productively, appreciate a thorough investigation. Unbiased and thorough investigations usually come to the correct conclusions.

At the conclusion of the investigation, the fact-finders will submit their findings to a company decision-maker. The company decision-maker will then review the facts, as determined by the investigators, and draw a conclusion as to whether sexual harassment occurred. If sexual harassment did occur, the company will have to decide on and implement appropriate discipline for the harasser as well as appropriate remedial action for the victim.

Remedies

If the company determines that illegal harassment has taken place, it has a duty to remedy the situation. The employer should stop the harassment and make sure that it does not recur. Disciplinary measures should be proportionate to the offense up to and including discharge. The company must also correct the effects of any harassment. For example, it can restore leave taken due to the harassment, erase negative evaluations, reinstate promotions or job duties, etc.

If the victim does not receive proper redress through the company's internal procedures, he or she can file a claim with the Equal Employment Opportunity Commission (EEOC) at the federal level, or the equivalent state agency – for example, the Department of Fair Employment and Housing (DFEH) in California – and one of those administrative agencies will investigate the claim. First, the agency will send a letter to the employer informing it of your claim and giving the employer a chance to respond. The agency may conduct a more thorough investigation or they may not. The limited resources of these agencies prevent them for fully investigating and adjudicating every claim they receive. However, you must file a claim with either the federal or state agency before you are allowed to take the claim to court. This procedure is known as exhausting your administrative remedies which you must do before advancing your claim to the court system. Once the agency has completed its investigation of a claim, it will then either take the case on behalf of the complaining employee or issue the employee a right-to-sue letter. Once an employee receives a right to sue letter, he or she can hire an attorney and sue the company in court for monetary damages.

CHAPTER 8

TOOLS FOR MANAGERS

Personal Liability For Sexual Harassment

Although not necessarily true in many states and under federal law, in California, supervisors are personally liable for any sexual harassment in which they engage or allow to happen. Therefore, we are not just talking about a financial hit to the company's balance sheet if sexual harassment occurs, but to personal pocketbooks in states like California. For example, Astra USA agreed to pay the victims of company sexual harassment $9.85 million and then sued about 30 of its employees for taking part in the harassment. Astra also sued its former CEO, who had participated in perpetrating the harassment, for $15 million to recover the costs of the investigation and settlement of the sexual harassment claims. So, individuals can incur the expenses of hiring an attorney and paying damages to the plaintiff and/or the company if they sexually harass someone or allow it to happen on their watch.

Therefore, be very careful about the behaviors you exhibit at work. Make sure that you are acting in a professional manner at all times. Know your duties and your company policies. Abide by company policy and the constraints of human decency at all times. Refrain from dating subordinates or at least do so fully aware of the huge risk you are taking.

If you were raised that certain behaviors are acceptable, rethink that upbringing in light of company policy and the law as previously described. You must set a high standard for yourself and others at work.

The Supervisor's Duty to Keep the Work Environment Harassment-Free

Employees enjoy the right to work in an environment that is free from discriminatory harassment. That means co-workers and supervisors can't harass each other. However, it also means that third parties can't harass workers either.

When clients, repair people, messengers or delivery people, for example, come into the workplace, they may make comments or exhibit inappropriate behavior. You may wonder how you can be expected to control their behavior. However, members of management must do what they can to prevent third party harassment. As a supervisor, you are responsible for maintaining a harassment-free workplace. That includes prohibiting harassment from third parties who are not employees of the company.

Even if the harassment is coming from an important client, and your company might lose that account if you say something to the client about his or her behavior, your obligation is to stop the harassment. Perhaps you can arrange a confidential meeting with the client to express your concerns in-person. Maybe you can gently convey your obligations and expectations to the client. However you do it, you must protect your employees. The post office will refuse to deliver mail to a house with a ferocious dog that puts the mail carrier at risk. You can and should refuse to service clients that put your employees at risk of sexual harassment. If the offender is a messenger, call his or her employer and tell them to send another messenger.

Continually monitor the workplace to ensure that all employees feel comfortable and valued. If you see something that strikes you as potentially offensive, address it. Either take it down, ask that the behavior stop, or inquire as to whether anyone was offended. Make sure any conversations you have in dealing with potential harassment issues are handled confidentially. Do not ask someone in front of others if they found something offensive. That puts them on the spot and may make them uncomfortable. When people feel uncomfortable, they sometimes also feel harassed.

Remember that the law is simply a floor for behavior, not a ceiling. If you strive for three things in your workplace: 1) awareness; 2) respect; 3) professionalism, you shouldn't need to worry about the law. Be aware of the feelings and reactions of others. If they seem unhappy, ask if there is anything you, as their supervisor, can do to help. Respect their answers. Employees these days come from very different backgrounds and cultures. Things they hold dear may seem insignificant to you. However, you must respect their feelings and make proactive efforts to maintain a harmonious workplace despite cultural differences. As a supervisor, it is your job to find a way for everyone to work together in harmony. Set an example for your employees through your professionalism. Always focus on the job at hand. How can employees do their jobs in a way that works for the entire organization? Make sure that you are always working to the highest professional standards and encourage your subordinates to follow your example.

Receiving Complaints

Employees have a right to complain to management of harassment or discrimination. In fact, you want to encourage them to do so. An open door policy along with prompt and correct action to end the problem is the company's and individual managers' first line of defense against legal problems related to discrimination. If you are proactive in addressing issues you see, you will have established a work environment where employees should feel free to come to you with their concerns.

Now, what do you do when someone comes in and tells you that they have been harassed? Listen compassionately and do not pass judgment. Do not say, "Oh, that couldn't have happened," or "I'm so sorry that happened." Both of those comments indicate that you do or do not believe the allegations. You need to remain completely neutral when receiving the complaint. Avoid comments like, "I've known Joe for years, and I just can't picture that!" Please don't say, "I don't believe it!" Don't indicate whether you do or do not believe it. Try not to pass judgment at all! Just get the facts and let the employee know that you have heard their complaint.

A good way to make employees feel heard is to validate them as they go along. How do you validate without sounding like you're agreeing with them? Every once in a while you say, "So, you just said, ' . . .'" and repeat what you've heard without any commentary of your own. They will either tell you you've got it right, and then continue, or they will correct you. If they correct you, it's a good thing you checked. If they say you're right, they are acknowledging that you actually heard what they were trying to tell you.

If you find an employee repeating themselves over and over, you have not done a good job of validating. People repeat themselves to make sure that they are being heard. When you finally validate their points, the repetition will stop. You can begin your validation with phrases such as, "So let me see if I understand you correctly. You just said . . ." You can also say, "So, as I understand it . . ." Phrases like that do not pass judgment. However, do not say things like, "I think it's horrible that . . ." or ". . . should never have happened." Those types of phrases indicate that you have taken a side or already made a decision as to the truth of the complaint.

Remember that the complaint will be investigated, and until the company determines what actually happened, you can't assume anything. Consider yourself the guardian of a process and not an advocate for either side. The process includes receiving the complaint and getting it through the complaint procedure in an appropriate manner. You may need to talk to the accused, so it's crucial to maintain your neutrality throughout the process.

Once you have heard the entire complaint and validated the

complainant, explain the rest of the complaint procedure. Usually, the next step will be to contact someone in Human Resources and they will start an investigation. Inform the complainant of what will happen next. Remind him or her that all complaints will be kept as confidential as possible by the company. However, **do not promise absolute confidentiality**. If the complaint is investigated, it will be talked about. However, the investigators should do this in as confidential a manner as possible.

Remind the complainant of the company's policy against discrimination and harassment. Tell them the company is committed to upholding the policy and that you will personally stay on top of the progression of the complaint. Then, make sure you do so. You might like to just hand off the complaint to Human Resources and consider yourself done with it. However, in one case a manager was held personally liable because he didn't check to make sure that Human Resources was pursuing the matter and the complaint was not resolved appropriately. Therefore, check back with both Human Resources and the complainant at least every other day until the complaint is fully resolved. Do this by phone or e-mail even if you are out of the office. (The manager held liable for not checking was on vacation for two weeks, but the court held him liable anyway.) Make sure that the company is consistently working toward resolution of the complaint and that the complainant knows the status of such efforts.

Duty to Guard Against Retaliation

Since retaliation claims raise an additional legal risk, take steps to avoid such claims every time you receive a complaint. Before the complainant leaves your office, make sure that you explain the company's policy against retaliation. Tell the complainant to come to you immediately if s/he feels retaliated against in any way for having filed this complaint.

Practically speaking, although you and the company may go to great lengths to keep all complaints confidential, news will still likely leak out anyway. You must guard against rumors. In some situations, people will side with the accused. When that happens, they may stop talking to the complainant. This can be construed as retaliation for filing the complaint. Rumors may embarrass the complainant, causing a claim of retaliation. Rumors may also harm an actually innocent accused giving rise to a possible defamation claim.

These things are hard for you to control, but you must try. Keep your ears and eyes open. If you see or hear anything that negatively impacts the complainant as a result of the complaint, address it immediately. You may have to hold a department meeting, issue a memo and have private chats with people. Do whatever it takes.

Certainly, don't allow anyone to take a negative employment action against the complainant as a result of the complaint. Watch that the complainant's duties, shifts, desk location, vacation approvals, etc. don't negatively change as a result of the complaint. Make sure that everyone is treated fairly and according to the same policies. Remember that discrimination is differential treatment. If everyone is treated the same way, there is no discrimination.

What to do if You are Accused of Sexual Harassment

If someone accuses you of sexual harassment, you may feel tempted to go on the defensive. Try to back up and look at the claim objectively. Could someone have construed your actions as offensive or inappropriate? Were you acting completely professionally? If you feel the claim could have resulted from a misunderstanding, you may want to learn from the situation, admit your mistake, and apologize to the complainant.

Even if you believe you are completely innocent and that the complainant is imagining or fabricating things, you must cooperate fully in any investigation and act professionally at all times. Tell the whole truth when questioned. Check your files for relevant documentation that can substantiate your version of the events. Do not discuss the claim outside the confines of the investigation process. If you start discussing the accusation in an attempt to build allies, you may find yourself liable for defamation or other legal claims. At the very least, you will have violated company policy providing for confidential handling of employee complaints.

Perhaps most importantly, watch that you take no action that anyone could construe as retaliatory against the complainant or anyone involved in the investigative process. As difficult as it may be, if the complainant is your subordinate, you cannot stop talking to him or her. You still have to communicate with the complainant in order for both of you to do your jobs. Make sure that you maintain a professional relationship with all those involved in the complaint or investigation. Refrain from taking any kind of employment action that will affect the complainant during the investigation, and make sure that any subsequent employment actions taken with respect to the complainant have appropriate supporting documentation and a compelling business justification. Even if the complainant is a poor performer, you cannot penalize him or her for poor performance without records documenting a sound basis for the penalty.

Again, if you document one person for poor attendance, make sure you are documenting all employees on attendance or whatever the issue may be. Even if one person sticks out in your mind as a problem, singling out an individual when others are also guilty (though to a lesser degree) can trigger a discrimination or retaliation claim.

CHAPTER 9

OTHER STEPS TO CORRECT OR PREVENT HARASSMENT CLAIMS

Always correct harassment whether or not a complaint is filed. If you see graffiti containing racial, ethnic, sexual, or any kind of slurs, remove it immediately. If you see inappropriate posters, take them down.

Dress Codes and Grooming Standards

A question usually arises about people who show up to work in "provocative" attire. If your company has a dress code, it should uniformly (pun intended) enforce that code, and employees should abide by it. Does low-cut or tight clothing give employees the license to harass? Of course not. However, your company's dress code should be designed to ensure professionalism and safety in the work environment. Employers can and should address clothing issues on that basis.

Make sure that you apply the same standards to men and women in your workplace. Employers may not refuse to allow employees to wear pants on the basis of sex unless:

- The employer has a "good cause exemption" formally granted by the California Fair Employment and Housing Commission (or equivalent state agency); or
- The outfit required is necessary to the job such as a costume would be for dramatic roles or specific character portrayal.

If an employee shows up at work dressed inappropriately for the workplace and in violation of the established policy, that employee should be sent home to change. They should be told that they are in violation of the dress code policy, not that they are asking to be harassed or that they are making others uncomfortable.

Some states have recently passed laws which allow hair styles representative of an employee's race, culture, or natural origin, such as California's CROWN Act.[24] This law expands the definition of race to include "traits historically associated with race, including, but not limited to, hair texture and protective hairstyles."[25] A similar bill has also been introduced at the federal level. So, employers should no longer require certain hairstyles of employees unless prompted by business necessity such as long, flowing hair that could get caught in machinery. Employers must also allow religious head covering absent a showing of legitimate business necessity.

Creating a Culture Which Avoids and Prevents Harassment

Creating a company culture intolerant of harassment starts at the top. If top company officials do not set the proper tone or if they engage in harassment themselves, then the rank and file will follow their bad examples. Top executives or business owners must demonstrate their commitment to inclusive and fair workplaces for all their employees, and develop a sense of urgency about it. Company leaders can do this by issuing company-wide statements, as well as

---

[24] CA SB 188 (2019) found at
https://leginfo.legislature.ca.gov/faces/billTextClient.xhtml?bill_id=201920200SB188 (Last visited 5/8/2020).
[25] CA Government Code Section 12926 (w).

personally and visibly attending anti-harassment training. Showing that the issue is worth their time and attention, sends a message that handling harassment concerns properly is a core company value worthy of the entire organization's time and resources.

Company leaders can also consistently order company climate surveys and continually change policies and procedures to address any concerns raised in these assessments. Further, based on survey results, management should develop systems within the workplace which promote their values and reward correct behavior.

In this regard, companies should first revamp their hiring processes. Employers should screen applicants for supervisory jobs to see if they have a history of engaging in harassment. If they do, they will not fit within a company dedicated to inclusion and respect. Company expectations with respect to the attitudes of their employees should be made clear on all hiring notices and applications. During interviews, the culture and expectations of the organization should be discussed and applicants asked for examples of times when they have gone out on a limb for a value they hold dear or in defense of someone improperly treated. Make it clear, during the hiring process, that the employer will not tolerate harassment.

Once hired, employees should continue to be held accountable for creating and maintaining a workplace free from harassment. Build that value into performance evaluations. Reward those who have stepped up to effect needed change or have worked hard to maintain a harassment free environment. Conversely, if someone has not fostered an appropriate environment, that person should receive a bad performance review regardless of their other competencies. If you want managers to proactively challenge and correct the inappropriate behavior of their subordinates, reward those who do and demote those who don't. Don't continue to reward harassers just because they otherwise contribute to the bottom line. Overall, their behavior will cost the organization in terms of employee absenteeism, declined enthusiasm, turnover, and legal liability.

If an employee has engaged in harassment, he or she should

receive discipline commensurate with the offense. Some behavior may not warrant immediate termination, but egregious behavior may. Again, don't protect wrongdoers simply because they have brought in many customers, have a special skill set, or have a special relationship with you. You can find a replacement who will better fit your culture of respect.

When working to change culture, consider rewarding managers with increased reports of sexual harassment. This up-tick should indicate that manager has succeeded in establishing an open door policy promoting a secure environment in which employees can bring forward their concerns. When culturally correct behaviors (e.g., creating civil and respectful workplaces, promptly reporting and investigating harassment claims, aggressively managing employees involved in or not adequately responding to harassment) are rewarded, this illustrates the priorities of an organization's leadership.[26] Some large companies have demonstrated their commitment to ethical and respectful workplaces by placing orders only from other companies certified as committed to the same goals.[27]

Companies should also keep records of harassment complaints and check those records when a complaint is made or a hiring or promotion decision is contemplated. Such records should help reveal any patterns of harassment by the same individuals. Those records may also indicate a need to rearrange the workplace.

Sometimes an office configuration can aid would-be harassers when vulnerable workers are isolated from others. In these situations, no one can witness the harassment or step in to help the victim. If you find such a situation, consider moving the victimized employee to a more visible work station, one where his or her interactions with others, especially supervisors, can be monitored.

---

[26] Report of the Select Task Force of the Study of Sexual Harassment in the Workplace, EEOC 2017 found at https://www.eeoc.gov/select-task-force-study-harassment-workplace#_Toc453686309 (Last visited 5/8/20).
[27] *Id.*

Establishing Clear and Complete Sexual Harassment Policies and Complaint Procedures

A good sexual harassment policy will include the following elements:

1. A statement that sexual harassment is illegal and that includes all current categories protected from discrimination in the employer's state.
2. A statement that sexual harassment is not tolerated by the company whether from employees or outside third parties.
3. The legal definition of sexual harassment.
4. Examples of behavior which can constitute sexual harassment. (See Appendix A) which includes a statement that mistreating other employees on social media carries the weight of any other workplace interaction.
5. A statement prohibiting retaliation against anyone bringing a claim or participating in the complaint process or investigation of a complaint.
6. A complaint procedure with multiple avenues for complaint.
7. A statement that any complaints will be handled as confidentially as possible, through an unbiased, timely investigation by qualified investigators.
8. The remedies available for sexual harassment.
9. How and where to report sexual harassment.
10. If 10 percent or more of your employees speak a language other than English as their spoken language, the employer should translate the policy into that language for those employees.

With respect to number six, a complaint procedure with multiple avenues of complaint, carefully determine whom to designate as complaint recipients. The idea here is to avoid forcing a victim to report the behavior to the harasser. So, victims must have more than one option. However, listing every supervisor as someone who can receive a complaint can open the employer up to unnecessary liability. Instead, choose several people in high positions of authority within the company as the ones designated to receive complaints. Then, train them how to receive such complaints and what to do once they have received a complaint. Choose individuals who are approachable, open, and committed to the anti-harassment values of the organization. Also, pick those who have some authority to do something about the complaint or to see that something is done about the complaint. If you pick members of higher management and they show their commitment to these roles, employees will further believe in the organization's commitment to a culture free from harassment.

Larger organizations might consider the use of ombudsmen, multi-lingual hotlines or web-based complaint systems. Not all organizations can support such systems. However, when creating reporting mechanisms, give employees access to someone who speaks their first or most comfortable language as well as someone geographically accessible to the complainant.

Remember that many employees now communicate through social media and texting. Anti-harassment policies should clarify that interactions, with other employees or which reference other employees on social media or through texting, fall within the company policy. Supervisors and others with anti-harassment responsibilities should especially watch their social media interactions with employees.

Make sure that whoever is appointed to investigate the complaint is competent to do so and is unbiased as well as perceived as unbiased with respect to the complainant, the accused and the organization. It is often difficult to achieve the perception of fairness if an internal employee conducts the investigation. In these cases, consider hiring an outside investigator competent and legally allowed to conduct workplace harassment investigations. Some states limit who can legally conduct workplace investigations. For example, California only allows internal employees, licensed private investigators or licensed attorneys acting in their capacity as attorneys to conduct workplace investigations.[28]

Employers must also start and complete investigations in a timely manner. The amount of time an investigation should take will vary according to the facts of each case. However, courts will not like unwarranted delays or evidence that shows the employer did not consider the complaint urgent. The investigations must also be thorough, and the accused must have a chance to respond to the allegations. For more on how to conduct workplace investigations, see my book, *Investigating the Workplace Harassment Complaint.*[29]

Once you have established your policy and complaint procedure, make sure that employees know the policy and how to access the complaint procedure. Provide training about the policy and continue to communicate it frequently to employees to maintain its visibility. Make sure that employees have easy access to the policy and complaint procedure any time they may want to reference it.

Training

In addition to training your employees about your company's specific anti-harassment policy and complaint procedure, organizations should provide company-wide compliance training designed to teach employees the behavior expected of them in the workplace. The most effective training is conducted live and tailored to the specific workplace. Different versions of the training should be developed for the rank and file employees and for managers.

Rank and file employees should receive training as to what legally constitutes harassment as well as what does not. Simply being asked to complete assignments on time or to come to work regularly does not, in itself, constitute harassment. Nor do genuine

---

[28] CA Business and Professions Code Section 7520 et seq.
[29] *Investigating the Workplace Harassment Complaint,* Beth K. Whittenbury, American Bar Association Publishing (2013) available on Amazon at https://www.amazon.com/Investigating-Workplace-Harassment-Claim-Whittenbury/dp/161438729X/ref=sr_1_1?dchild=1&keywords=Beth+K.+Whittenbury&qid=1588994698&sr=8-1.

compliments. However, any behaviors that stand in for the A, B or C in our equations explained in chapter four, should be avoided in the workplace. Effective training will use examples applicable to the given workplace and ask participants to apply the concepts taught to those scenarios.

Managers will likely need longer training sessions which cover not only the material taught to the rank and file, but also explain their duty to prevent and remedy sexual harassment of which the managers become aware. Managers need to understand the potential for both company and personal liability if sexual harassment occurs on their watch. Managers should also understand the full range of remedies and disciplines available in cases of verified sexual harassment.

Some states such as California, Connecticut, and Maine, among others, require sexual harassment training. Each state may differ in the length and coverage of the required training. California's training law now requires trainers to cover the topic of abusive conduct in the workplace in addition to illegal harassment. So, check the laws in your jurisdiction to make sure that your company is complying with local training laws.

In addition, there is a move toward civility and bystander training in companies committed to creating cultures free from harassment, intimidation, or bullying in the workplace. Civility training focuses on promoting respect and civility in the workplace generally and does not focus on the legality or illegality of behavior. Bystander training empowers employees to support each other or to intervene when witnessing harassment of a co-worker. This type of training teaches employees to recognize undesirable behavior, creates a collective sense of responsibility to step in and take action, generates a feeling of empowerment to do something about undesirable behavior, and provides bystanders with resources they can call on to support their interventions.

CHAPTER 10

OTHER ISSUES TO CONSIDER

In addition to sex or gender, the law protects other categories from discrimination/harassment. As a supervisor, you should know that the California Fair Employment and Housing Act (FEHA), one of the most comprehensive of these laws, protects individuals from discrimination or harassment based on the following characteristics.

- Age (40 and over)
- Ancestry
- Color
- Religious creed
- Family and medical care leave (don't deny it under legally mandated terms)
- Disability (mental and physical) including HIV and AIDS
- Marital status
- Medical condition (i.e. cancer, genetic characteristics, etc.)
- National origin
- Race
- Religion
- Sex (including pregnancy, breastfeeding, childbirth, and related medical conditions)

- Sexual orientation (including transgender issues)
- Gender expression/identity
- Military or veteran status
- Political activities or affiliation
- Victims of stalking, sexual assault, and domestic violence

Please be aware that supervisors should not allow any employee to experience work-related harassment due to any of these categories. Although some of these categories are not protected under federal law, it is best to work with the most inclusive list available. Even if a category such as appearance is not on this list, remember that treating people differently from others for any reason can lead to complaints. So, try to provide a level playing field for all regardless of any particular characteristic a person exhibits.

Transgender Issues

One area that managers find difficult to navigate with respect to harassment laws is the issue of transgender employees. Especially in cases where an employee is undergoing a gender transition, other employees sometimes say or do things that could constitute harassment toward the employee in gender transition.

Twenty-one states have recognized that discrimination against transgender and gender non-conforming people is a form of sex discrimination. Therefore, no one in the workplace should make comments or slurs relating to stereotypical notions of how men and women should act. The conduct does not need to be sexual in nature to constitute sexual harassment. For example, you should not negatively comment on the way someone dresses, wears their hair or walks, because such comments can give rise to harassment claims.

Employees have the right to decide with which gender they will affiliate. Most officials suggest that employers allow employees to use the bathroom that fits their gender choice. Public restroom use is governed by a legal patchwork of city ordinances and state laws. San

Francisco, Oakland, and New York have regulations protecting public restroom access based on "gender identity." "Gender identity" refers to a person's internal sense of gender rather than their birth sex. Where possible, establish an "all gender" bathroom on your premises to avoid these issues in your workplace. An "all gender" bathroom is one lockable room with a toilet and wash basin that can be used by either gender, but just by one person at a time. Name this an "all gender" restroom. As of this writing, no employee can be forced to use an all gender restroom where gender specific restrooms are available and employees can choose which gender specific restroom best conforms to their gender identity.

When watching for transgender discrimination issues, remember that discharge, demotion, refusal to hire, transfer to a less desirable position, failure to use appropriate names, pronouns and titles, failure to allow bathroom use according to gender identity and harassment by co-workers, supervisors or management among others can all give rise to a harassment claim.

English Only Rules

Sometimes managers feel frustrated if their employees can communicate among themselves in a language other than English. However, employers, at least in California, cannot force employees to speak English in the workplace unless the employer can show that speaking English is a business necessity. Supervisors can ask that employees speak only English with them, if that is the only language the supervisors know, but they cannot ban employees from speaking with each other in a different language unless that causes danger to others or serious interference with legitimate business objectives. If an employer has a legitimate reason for banning all languages other than English during certain times, it must notify employees in advance of enforcing that language policy. If employees are not notified in advance of the policies, then those policies cannot be used as a basis for discipline.

Appendix A

Guidelines for Recognizing Sexual Harassment

Ask yourself the following questions to determine whether certain behavior is sexual harassment.

1. Would you want your child, parent, sibling, or spouse to endure the situation?

2. Is the behavior job-related? Is it focused on getting the job done?

3. Is the behavior directed toward only women or only men?

4. Can the behavior be classified as courting, flirting, or other sexual behavior?

5. Has the employee receiving the attention objected to the behavior in any way?

6. Has the behavior happened before?

7. Does the behavior make it more difficult for the receiving employee to do his or her job?

8. Would a reasonable person of the same gender as the recipient feel demeaned, degraded, or embarrassed by the behavior?

9. Is someone using a position of power to make a person of the opposite gender feel inferior, vulnerable or victimized?

10. Is a supervisor predicating job-related status on receptivity to sexual advances?

11. Has behavior toward an employee changed negatively because the employee reported incidents of sexual harassment or participated in an investigation of alleged sexual harassment?

Types of Behavior that May be Considered Sexual Harassment Depending on Their Severity and Frequency (the more severe the less frequency required)

PHYSICAL:

- Touching

- Holding

- Grabbing

- Pinching

- Hugging

- Kissing

- Patting

- Poking

- Brushing against another employee's body

- Impeding or blocking movement

- "Accidental" collisions

- Other unwanted contact

- Physical assault

- Rape

VERBAL:

- Offensive jokes

- Offensive language

- Threats

- Sexual comments

- Sexual suggestions

- Offensive sounds

- Teasing of a sexual nature

- Sexual propositions

- Whistling

- Continuing to express personal interest after being informed the interest is unwelcome

NONVERBAL:

- Staring at a person's body or body parts

- Leaning over someone at a desk

- Offensive gestures or motions

- Circulating letters or cartoons

- Display of sexually suggestive objects, posters, calendars, graffiti

- Other sexually oriented behavior

Note: This list is not all inclusive. It is merely designed to present examples and guidelines.

Appendix B

Some Specific Actions Cited in Cases That Can Constitute Sexual Harassment

- Managers putting knives to the throats of teenage female employees
- Placing employees in police-style restraint holds
- Comments on the bodies of and leering at employees and/or customers
- Repeated inquiries as to whether employees would have sex with customers
- Inappropriate touching
- Use of extreme profanity
- Promotion of supervisors who engaged in above-listed activities
- Stalking-type behavior
- Persistent requests for dates
- Pornographic photographs in the workplace
- Obscene jokes
- Sexual propositions
- Groping
- Sexual assault

Beth K. Whittenbury

Appendix C

Answers and Explanations to Vignettes

Vignette 1: If you said that Sally could file a hostile environment sexual harassment claim based on the facts, you answered correctly. We can eliminate a quid pro quo claim because the facts did not include any kind of employment decision. Although most women within the organization might view their chances for promotion within that department dismal at best, so far, under the facts given, no one has been denied a promotion based on gender.

Let's review the elements necessary for a sexual harassment claim. First, was there sexual conduct? Now, you may be thinking that there was nothing sexual at all in this vignette. That's true. However, remember that we made the point earlier that for the "sexual conduct" element we are looking first and foremost for a gender distinction, because sexual harassment is a form of sex discrimination. Here, the department head clearly makes a distinction between men and women.

Note that I did not identify the gender of the department head. Does it matter? No. The courts recognize both male-on-male and female-on-female sexual harassment where the plaintiff can prove a gender distinction. Sometimes female managers have a low estimation of their own gender, themselves excluded perhaps. However, if a woman makes the workplace intolerable for other women, but not men, then we have met our sexual conduct element.

Next, was the sexual conduct, the repetitious comments, unwelcome to Sally? It would be hard to imagine Sally appreciating those comments, so it's probably safe to say that they were unwelcome to her since even by an objective standard they would be unwelcome to all women wishing to advance in the workplace.

Finally, for hostile environment, we need to find that a reasonable woman in the same set of circumstances would find that these repetitious comments create a hostile or offensive working environment. Would a reasonable woman feel that there was no hope for advancement in this department? I think most of us would agree that's exactly how she'd feel, especially when humiliated in front of clients during a presentation.

So, it appears that this vignette meets all the requirements of a hostile environment claim. Would Sally actually win in court? That would depend on the jury chosen. However, you can clearly see how this department head is putting the company and him or herself at risk of a lawsuit though this behavior.

Vignette 2: Here we have unwelcome, sexual conduct. The dirty jokes are the sexual conduct and Al has made it clear to Fresia that it is unwelcome coming from her. Remember that Al has the right to appreciate conduct from one person and not from another. Here, he's okay with his friend Robert telling him dirty jokes, but he doesn't like it from Fresia. That's his prerogative, but in some jurisdictions he does have an obligation to make that clear to Fresia, which he does.

Now, if you are a supervisor who is aware of this situation, you should take advantage of this opportunity to show employees both that you know and uphold company policies. Take Fresia aside and let her know that you witnessed the interchange. Remind her of the company sexual harassment policies and make it clear to her that since Al has requested she stop that behavior toward him, that she must stop. Let her know that you will also be talking to Al and asking him to let you know if there are any further incidents like this between the two of them.

Then talk to Al. Let him know that you overheard the interchange and have already spoken to Fresia. Ask him to let you know if she tells him any further dirty jokes because you have now directly asked her not to do so. You may also let Al and Robert know that it would be best for them to refrain from telling such jokes at work, since it is clearly sending the wrong message to employees. Clearly Fresia overheard them, so others could too. Just because Fresia seemed to welcome the jokes doesn't mean that they might not be offending others. It's best if they limit such friendly discussions to their own time off company property.

Although this incident is at too low a level to warrant placing any type of formal reprimand in anyone's file, make sure an HR representative is told about it. This time you overheard it, but next time a different supervisor or employee may. If there is no central clearinghouse for incidents that allows the company to keep track, this could go on for quite some time without the company realizing that each time is not the first time, but instead is part of a series of events noticed by different people each time.

Vignette 3: This looks like a potential case of quid pro quo sexual harassment – right? We clearly have the "tangible employment action" – she was fired. However, let's go through all the elements.

First, was there sexual conduct? Clearly, yes there was between the two doctors. They had a sexual affair. Second, was the affair welcome? Here we don't really know, do we?

The first doctor is a former Chief of Staff. Clearly, he knows and has worked closely with the hospital's board members. He is likely held in high regard by the board. The new doctor has no track record with the board. She could have felt that things would go better with her at the hospital if she acquiesced to the wishes of the former Chief of Staff. If she raises this point and says that the affair was consensual, but not welcome, how can the Chief of Staff or the hospital prove otherwise? She can claim that she was afraid that if the relationship ended, her job would be jeopardized. In fact, it appears that is exactly what happened. Within a month of the relationship ending, she lost her job, clearly an employment decision and job detriment – the final element needed for a quid pro quo claim.

Even if the former Chief of Staff didn't ask the board to remove her because her presence made him uncomfortable now that the relationship was over, how does the hospital prove a negative like that? The situation looks bad for the employer, and it's possible that all the criteria of a sexual harassment case exist, so, ultimately, a jury will decide. You can see how such a situation can end as a sexual harassment lawsuit.

Vignette 4: To have a legitimate retaliation claim, Ally must show that she first engaged in some form of protected activity. Now clearly, had Ally filed a complaint about her VP stating that he had asked her to do something illegal, filing that claim would have been "protected activity." However, Ally never made a complaint; she never even refused to fire the counter employee. All she ever said on the subject was to request a legitimate reason to fire the person. The cosmetic company's attorney could probably argue that Ally, in fact, didn't act at all. However, the court found that simply not acting when inaction is based on a reasonable belief that the requested action is illegal counts as "protected activity" under the law. Further, appearance is not a category protected from discrimination under the law, and one could argue that a cosmetics company has a legitimate business interest in their counter employee's appearance. Again, the court said that even though there is no actual law prohibiting appearance discrimination, most people would probably think one exists. Therefore, the court found that all the plaintiff needs to show in a retaliation case is a reasonable, good faith belief that he or she is acting in accordance with the law to meet the first criteria of a retaliation case, namely "protected activity."

Next, Ally needs to show an adverse action taken against her. Clearly, monitoring her expense reports while not doing that to anyone else, asking her subordinates for dirt on her, and lowering her performance ratings as a result qualify as adverse actions.

Finally, the court or jury must find a causal link between the protected activity and the adverse action for the plaintiff to establish a case for retaliation. Courts usually look for a close nexus in time between the protected activity and the adverse action to help establish this prong. In the vignette, the VP started auditing Ally's expense reports and talking to her subordinates shortly after she failed to fire the counter employee. The situation looks bad for the employer. Can they defend themselves at all?

If you understand this case as explained above, you see that the only place the employer can defend itself is with respect to the third and final prong – the causal connection criteria. However, as a supervisor, you can't control what's in someone else's head. Remember that one of the rules of this vignette is that the employee doesn't have to tell you that s/he thinks s/he is engaging in protected activity. So you simply can't defend yourself or the company based on that first prong. Next, as a manager, you will sometimes have to take adverse actions against your employees. When you do, make sure they deserve them. Before you make a decision that affects someone else negatively, ask yourself if you have a legitimate business justification for the decision. Picture yourself on the witness stand explaining your action to the jury. If you see them all nodding along with you, indicating that they would have done the same thing, then go ahead and make the decision, but document your reasons why it was justified by business reasons. If you imagine a jury looking confused, concerned, or even worse, angry, then you'd better re-think your decision.

The only place you can really defend yourself is on that last prong – the connection between the adverse action and the protected activity. To defend yourself there, make sure that there is no connection between any alleged protected activity and any adverse action you take against an employee by checking that instead you have a business reason for the action. For your sake and for the company's, every time you take an "adverse action" first write down the reasons for the decision. That way, if it's ever questioned, you are ready to explain it and don't have to search your own memory banks as to why you decided to do a certain thing on a certain day.

In the case on which I based the facts for this vignette, the VP did not have anything written down to justify his actions. The court felt that his actions looked like a "witch hunt" motivated by the fact that Ally had refused to fire the counter employee. The court allowed the case to go to trial, finding that Ally had made out her basic case for retaliation and it was up to the jury to determine the facts. (The names of the parties have been changed and the facts adapted to make the points in this vignette.)

Vignette 5: Here, the two employees clearly engaged in protected activity when they filed the sexual harassment complaint. Bringing a complaint, participating in an ensuing investigation, and even the state of being a potential witness in an investigation are considered protected activity.

Was there an adverse action? Remember our definition: something that would dissuade a reasonable worker from filing a harassment or discrimination claim in the future. Do you think that filing a claim only to have a private investigator start asking your family and co-workers embarrassing questions about you would dissuade others from coming forward with complaints in the future? Most of us probably would. The court in this case agreed and found that even though the investigator misunderstood his orders from the company and the company probably didn't intend to authorize such a response, the background check happened and as such constituted an adverse action on the part of the company against those employees who had complained. Once again, there is no motive requirement for retaliation. The only question is whether the adverse action occurred, not whether the company intended it to.

This case illustrates that "adverse actions" as part of a retaliation claim differs somewhat from the "tangible employment actions" element in quid pro quo cases. In this vignette, the adverse action did not affect the men's employment. They still kept their jobs, shifts, salaries, etc. However, they were adversely affected by the company's action in their personal lives. So, you can see that "adverse action" is much broader than "tangible employment actions."

Finally, it is clear that there was a causal connection between the men's sexual harassment complaints and the company's adverse action. But for the men filing the complaint, the company would not have asked the P.I. to conduct an investigation. So, the final answer is: yes – the men would have all the elements of a retaliation case under this vignette.

Appendix D

Frequently Asked Questions

Q: Is it bad to date a subordinate?

A: *It's risky because you can't prove that it was welcome after the fact.*

Q: If I'm finding a problem with an employee, can I start documenting his or her behavior?

A: *Yes, as long as you also document all others exhibiting the same behavior. If you single someone out for documentation, this can be considered discrimination.*

Q: Can calendars or pin-ups displayed at work, in lockers, or in a warehouse area be considered sexual harassment?

A: *Yes. Such displays may contribute to a hostile working environment.*

Q: Can I ask a co-worker out on a date?

A: *Yes, but if you receive any indication that similar future requests are unwelcome, do not ask again. If the co-worker refuses your first invitation, you probably should not ask again.*

Q: If no one in our organization is complaining of sexual harassment, how can we have a problem?

A: *Often sexual harassment goes unreported in organizations because employees are too embarrassed or afraid to mention the problem to a supervisor or human resources representative. Employees also fail to report sexual harassment out of a reluctance to get another employee in trouble. However, these situations may escalate and lead to lawsuits if not discovered and handled early.*

Q: Can comments made by customers to my employees constitute sexual harassment?

A: *Yes. An employer may be liable for sexual harassment done to their employees by people who are not their employees when the harassment occurs in the line of work, the employer knows or should have known about it and the employer fails to take immediate and appropriate action.*

Q: If a co-worker wears provocative clothing, is he or she asking for trouble?

A: *No. Everyone has the right to work in an environment free from sexual harassment. However, the way someone acts or dresses may be an indication of whether or not they view some conduct as unwelcome. The more provocative the dress, the clearer the employee must state that they find certain conduct offensive and unwelcome.*

Q: If a worker goes along with my sexual jokes or also uses foul language, am I immune from a sexual harassment claim from that employee?

A: *No, not necessarily. Whereas, the court may take the alleged victim's behavior into account as a factor to help determine if the behavior was unwelcome, joining in jokes, or use of foul language by the alleged victim, is not a defense to a claim of quid pro quo or hostile environment sexual harassment, nor does it excuse or invite extreme or abusive environmental behavior.*

Q: Can someone who has been in a consensual sexual relationship file a sexual harassment complaint after the consent has been withdrawn?

A: *Yes, if the person has clearly withdrawn consent to the relationship and harassment begins and continues in the face of refusals, the person being harassed may file a sexual harassment claim. Under these circumstances, the victim should communicate clear refusals to the alleged harasser and report the harassment.*

Q: Aren't most reports of sexual harassment untrue or grossly exaggerated?

A: *No. Very few actual reports of sexual harassment have been found to be false.*

Q: If one employee submits to sexual requests by a supervisor and gains benefits from the submission, can another employee sue the employer for sexual discrimination?

A: *Yes. Other employees who were equally qualified and denied benefits may sue for sexual discrimination.*

Q: Is the company liable for sexual harassment done by supervisors of which it is unaware, even if the company has a posted policy against sexual harassment?

A: *Yes. The company is vicariously liable for "quid pro quo" (this for that) sexual harassment and the supervisor may be personally liable depending on state law.*

Q: If no one corroborates the alleged victim's report, can I still discipline the alleged harasser?

A: *Yes. The EEOC does not require corroboration of sexual harassment charges. The employer must take the action it deems most appropriate after weighing the credibility of the parties.*

Q: What are the remedies for sexual harassment?

A: *The first remedy is to use the company's internal complaint procedure as outlined in your company handbook and discussed during your training. If that procedure fails to remedy the harassment, an employee can refer the case to the appropriate state agency or the EEOC.*

Q: As a manager, what do I do if I am personally accused of harassment?

A: *Cooperate fully in any investigation. Tell the truth. Watch that you take no action that may be perceived as retaliation against the person filing the complaint or anyone participating in the investigation. Check your files for all relevant documentation that will substantiate your version of events.*

Appendix E - Quiz Yourself

Test Questions

For the following questions please answer T (true) or F (false)

1. If I am accused of sexual harassment, I should stop speaking or interacting with my accuser under all circumstances until the situation is resolved.
   T   F

2. The three elements of quid pro quo or tangible employment action harassment are: 1) unwelcome 2) sexual conduct 3) that is so severe and pervasive that it creates a hostile working environment. T   F

3. Giving an employee different tasks within the same job description can be considered adverse action in a retaliation case. T   F

4. The company must conduct an investigation into any allegation or inference of sexual harassment in order to gather the facts and fashion an appropriate remedy where necessary.
   T   F

5. Supervisors should have an open door policy for receiving complaints of sexual harassment. T   F

6. Sexual harassment is a form of gender discrimination. T   F

7. You should always guarantee absolute confidentiality to an employee complaining of sexual harassment. T   F

8. If I see something questionable, but no one complains, as a supervisor, I don't have to do anything. T   F

9. The company is not responsible when co-workers ostracize an employee who has filed a sexual harassment complaint. T   F

10. In California, supervisors are personally liable for their own acts of sexual harassment as well as the acts of subordinates that they knowingly allow. T   F

11. The company is strictly liable (automatically liable) for hostile environments created by co-workers. T   F

12. When an employee comes to you with a complaint, you should agree with them immediately. T   F

13. Once you have forwarded a complaint to HR or a higher authority, you have done your job and can forget about it. T   F

14. There is no risk to having a romantic relationship with a subordinate as long as it is consensual. T   F

15. If the harasser is a client and not an employee, I don't have to do anything. T   F

16. I should remain neutral when receiving a complaint even if I think it's a false claim. T   F

17. Dirty jokes sent around the company by e-mail can never create a hostile environment claim. T   F

18. If someone has experienced sexual harassment they do not need to report it internally or to an administrative agency before filing a lawsuit. T   F

19. If an employee does not receive satisfaction when filing an internal complaint with the company, they can then file a claim with the DFEH. T   F

20. The three things a plaintiff has to initially establish to bring a retaliation claim in court are: 1) protected activity; 2) adverse action; 3) a causal link between 1 and 2. T   F

21. A male employee can file a sexual harassment claim against another male employee. T   F

22. If an employee's concerns about sexual harassment seem unreasonable to you, you can ignore them. T   F

23. If an employer has a policy against sexual harassment, but fails to enforce it, the employer can use the "Avoidable Consequences Doctrine." T   F

24. A potential witness in a sexual harassment complaint cannot file a retaliation claim based on his or her potential witness status. T   F

25. Courts have recognized that discrimination against transgender and gender non-conforming people is a form of sex discrimination. T   F

Beth K. Whittenbury

QUIZ ANSWER KEY

1. False
2. False
3. True
4. True
5. True
6. True
7. False
8. False
9. False
10. True
11. False
12. False
13. False
14. False
15. False
16. True
17. False
18. False
19. True
20. True
21. True
22. False
23. False
24. False
25. True

Beth K. Whittenbury

ABOUT THE AUTHOR

Beth K. Whittenbury, J.D.

Beth K. Whittenbury has been an attorney since 1990. She began her legal career in the Labor and Employment Law Group of what was then the largest law firm in San Francisco. She left to found her consulting practice specializing in sexual harassment training, mediations, and investigations. Since 1993, she has dedicated herself to resolving employment issues without litigation. She now provides anti-discrimination and implicit bias training and helps employers create climates of respect, inclusivity and civility.

Ms. Whittenbury is active in the American Bar Association (ABA), the California Bar Association, the California Lawyers Association (CLA), and the Professionals in Human Resources Association ("PIHRA," the Southern California Chapter of the Society of Human Resources Management). She has served in numerous leadership roles within those organizations including as a CLA delegate to the ABA House of Delegates and is in line to chair a section of the ABA in the 2021-22 bar year.

Beth taught business law at the collegiate level for 5 years. She has written five books, numerous articles and appeared as a presenter, moderator, and keynote speaker for several major conferences. Her book: *Investigating the Workplace Harassment Claim*, available from ABA Publishing at www.ShopABA.org, made the ABA Best Seller's List. Her books have also been rated as Amazon Best Sellers in their categories.

Ms. Whittenbury has been recognized by her peers for her quality of professional service and high ethical standards, as evidenced by her election to the Fellows of the American Bar Foundation (ABF), the Civil Rights and Social Justice Committee Excellence Award, and the President's Volunteer Service Lifetime Achievement Award.

Beth K. Whittenbury

ACKNOWLEDGMENTS

The Author thanks her family without whose support this book would not appear in this form. She also posthumously thanks Tony Kulisch, Ph.D., a wonderful business partner, mentor, and friend who jointly devised the formulas stated herein. She also thanks everyone who works for social justice. May all our efforts find success!

Beth K. Whittenbury can be reached through her website:
www.bkwhittenbury.com

For more information or to hire

Beth K. Whittenbury, J.D.

as a speaker, to train your employees or to evaluate and improve your workplace culture

please visit

www.bkwhittenbury.com

More Books by Beth K. Whittenbury, J.D.

Investigating the Workplace Harassment Claim

A Manager's Guide to Preventing Liability for Sexual Harassment in the Workplace

The Education Bill of Rights: A Summary of Findings from the ABA Civil Rights and Social Justice Section's Education Focus Groups

AND

Award-winning children's picture book, *Just Love Him, I Guess,* which promotes responsible parenting.

For all books written by Beth K. Whittenbury, enter her name in the search bar at Amazon.com or visit her author page, www.BethWhittenbury.com

Beth K. Whittenbury

Beth K. Whittenbury

Beth K. Whittenbury

www.ingramcontent.com/pod-product-compliance
Lightning Source LLC
Chambersburg PA
CBHW060620200326
41521CB00007B/836